Triceratops on the Farm

Written by Sarah Hobhouse and David Mackay

Illustrated by Tony Ross

One day Wesley went on a school trip to a farm.

The children saw horses, ducks, sheep and pigs.

Wesley asked to have a go on the tractor.
The farmer helped him up.
"Look! The cows are coming to be milked,"
said the farmer.

Wesley saw a large dark animal with them.
It looked as if it had three horns.

Wesley thanked the farmer and jumped down.
He walked over to the gate.
"Looks just like a Triceratops,"
he said to himself.

Triceratops lumbered along, swishing its tail.
Hens ran flapping and clucking out of its way.

Triceratops snatched mouthfuls of leaves
and flowers from the hedge.

Its long horns shone in the sun.
A crow stood on its back.

It scratched itself against a tall tree.

Two squirrels ran up the tree
and hid in their nest.

Triceratops pawed the ground
and bits of earth flew all over the place.
Then it charged up the field towards the cows.

Triceratops marched round them.
"Triceratops!" called Wesley from the gate.

Triceratops looked up.
It walked over to Wesley.
Wesley climbed on the gate.
"Be careful!" shouted the farmer.
"That's the bull."

"I thought you were Triceratops,"
Wesley said quietly.
Then he jumped down and ran after his friends.

Triceratops

This dinosaur's name means Head With Three Horns.
Triceratops also had bony plates round its neck. It was
a plant eater.

If a Tyrannosaurus attacked it, Triceratops fought
back with its sharp horns. It was 6 metres long and
3 metres high – about as big as a single-decker bus.